LIFE OF RYAN...

AND RONNIE

Meic Povey

ISBN: 0–9543710-7-0

For permission to perform one of the plays published here, contact:
sgriptcymru, Chapter, Market Road, Canton, Cardiff, CF5 1QE.

Tel: 029 2023 6650
sgriptcymru@sgriptcymru.com
www.sgriptcymru.com

This play was commissioned and first performed by **sgrip**tcymru on 12 October 2005 in the Weston Studio, Wales Millennium Centre, Cardiff.

This book is published with the financial support of the Welsh Books Council.

CEFNOGI CREADIGRWYDD
CYNGOR CELFYDDYDAU CYMRU
THE ARTS COUNCIL OF WALES
SUPPORTING CREATIVITY

HUGH JAMES
SOLICITORS

Cover design and image: A1
Cover photo credit: Matt Wright
Typesetting: Eira Fenn
Printed in Wales by Cambrian Printers, Aberystwyth

LIFE OF RYAN... AND RONNIE

by

MEIC POVEY

Actors:

Ryan	Aled Pugh
Ronnie	Kai Owen

Director:	Simon Harris
Designer:	Max Jones
Lighting Designer:	Jeanine Davies
Sound Designer:	James Williams
Movement:	Stephen Fisher

Production Manager:	Sarah Cole
Company Stage Manager:	Richard Balshaw
Technical Stage Manager:	Jane Lalljee
Costume Supervisor:	Sue Jackson
Company Director:	Stephen Fisher
Assistant Director:	Arwel Gruffydd

Note: The text was correct at the time of going to press,
but it may have changed during rehearsals.

sgriptcymru
contemporarydramawales

sgriptcymru is the national company for contemporary drama in Wales, specialising in new writing by Welsh and Wales-based playwrights.

The company holds a pivotal role in discovering and promoting exciting new voices for the stage. **sgript**cymru is unique in its exclusive dedication to producing new writing in both Welsh and English. It is also a development organisation that works with emerging playwrights at the grass-roots level, as well as a commissioning company working with professional playwrights and offering rare freedom to their creativity.

Through **sgript**cymru's professional support to dramatists and its award-winning programme of new productions each year, the company aims to ensure the continuing existence of a new writing culture in Wales and to enhance its place in the wider world. The company has gained an enviable reputation for the quality and range of its work in theatres nationwide since its inception in 2000.

"The excellent new writing company"
The Guardian, June 2003

The Company:

Artistic Director	Simon Harris
Associate Director	Elen Bowman
Administrative Director	Mai Jones
Development Director	Emma Routledge
Literary Manager	Angharad Elen
Marketing Manager	Siân Melangell Dafydd
Marketing Assistant	Steffan Deiniol
Artistic Associate	Bethan Jones
Associate Writer	Meic Povey

The Board of Directors:
Ann Beynon (Chair), Frances Medley (Vice-Chair), Philippa Davies, Nicola Heywood-Thomas, Richard Houdmont, Elwyn Tudno Jones, David Seligman, Lucy Shorrocks, Hedd Vine, Elinor Williams, Mared Hughes (Associate Member).

Patrons:
Rakie Ayola
Russell T. Davies
Matthew Rhys
Amy Wadge

Cyhoeddiadau Dalier Sylw

sgriptcymru Publications

Available from:
sgriptcymru
Chapter, Market Road, Canton, Cardiff, CF5 1QE
Tel: 029 2023 6650
sgriptcymru@sgriptcymru.com
www.sgriptcymru.com

Playwright: Meic Povey

Born in 1950 in Snowdonia, north Wales and one of ten children, Meic started his professional career with Cwmni Theatr Cymru in 1968. He has been a freelance writer for over thirty years and is generally regarded as one of Wales' leading dramatists. His work for theatre, television and film includes: *Nos Sadwrn Bach*, *Aelwyd Gartrefol*, *Taff Acre*, *Meistres y Chwarae*; *Camau Troellog*, *Sul y Blodau*, *Deryn*, *Babylon By-Passed*, *Y Filltir Sgwâr*, *Christmas Story*, *Nel*, *Yr Ynys*, *Terfyn*, *Y Cadfridog*, *Chwara Plant*, *Gwaed Oer*, *Diwedd y Byd*, *Yr Hen Blant*, *Yn Debyg Iawn i Ti a Fi*, *Y Weithred*, *Wyneb yn Wyneb*, *Perthyn*, *Fel Anifail*, *Yr Heliwr*, *Bonansa!*, *Tair* and *Talcen Caled*.

Most recently, his work has included *Sylw* (Royal Welsh College of Music and Drama in association with **sgript**cymru, 2001), *Bob a'i Fam* for Welsh-language television channel S4C and the hugely successful *Indian Country*, his first English-language stage play, presented by **sgript**cymru on a national tour and at the Traverse Theatre in Edinburgh. In 2004, a revised version of Meic's play *Yn Debyg Iawn i Ti a Fi* was selected to be the first production of the newly created national theatre of Wales, Theatr Genedlaethol Cymru. Meic Povey is **sgript**cymru's Associate Writer. An English translation of his play *Tair* was recently presented by **sgript**cymru at the Traverse Theatre in Edinburgh and, as part of a prestigious collaboration with the Royal Shakespeare Company and the Union des Théâtres de L'Europe, is currently being published for performance in five major European languages. In 1991 Meic received his first BAFTA Wales best scriptwriter award for *Nel*; his second came in 2005 for *Talcen Caled*. He is currently working for TG4, the Irish-language TV station, as script editor and story consultant on a new drama comedy, *Paddywackery*.

Director: Simon Harris

Simon Harris is Artistic Director of **sgrip**cymru, which he helped create, and *Life of Ryan... and Ronnie* will be his sixth production for the company. Born and brought up in Swansea, Simon studied English at University College, London and trained at RADA. Previous productions for **sgrip**cymru include *Franco's Bastard* by Dic Edwards, *past away* by Tracy Harris and *Indian Country,* also by Meic Povey, which opened at Chapter Arts Centre, Cardiff, before touring Wales and being staged at the Traverse Theatre in Edinburgh to great acclaim. Subsequently, it won two awards in the Theatre in Wales Awards of 2003. Most recently, Simon has directed an award-winning production of Gary Owen's *Ghost City* which took the company to New York for the first time, and *Crossings* by Clare Duffy, which played in Wales, London and returned to Edinburgh. Other directing credits include *Forever Yours Marie Lou* (BAC), *Nothing to Pay* (BAC and tour), *The Dresser* (Plymouth Theatre Royal) and *Badfinger* (Donmar and tour). He has recently been selected as the first Welsh Fellow on the prestigious Clore Leadership Programme for 2005/06.

Aled Pugh (Ryan)

Aled trained at the Royal Welsh College of Music and Drama. His theatre credits there include *Hedda Gabler*, *Knives in Hens*, *A Family Affair* and *Macbeth*. Aled's other theatre credits include *Hamlet* (Theatre Royal Northampton), *Waiting for Godot* and *Portrait of the Artist as a Young Dog* (Clwyd Theatr Cymru), *The Golden Ass* and *A Midsummer Night's Dream* (Shakespeare's Globe) and *Erogenous Zones* (Sherman Theatre).

On television, Aled has appeared in *Red Cap*, *Lucky Bag*, *My Family*, *Unto the Wicked* (BBC), *The Secret Life of Michael Fry* (Channel 4) and *Cant y Cant*, *Rownd a Rownd* and *Hapus Dyrfa* (S4C). His radio credits include *Money for Old Rope*, *Making Waves*, *In Parenthesis* (Radio 4) and *Eileen* (Radio Cymru).

Kai Owen (Ronnie)

Kai was born and bred in Llanrwst and he trained at The Mountview Academy. Kai is an Associate Actor at Clwyd Theatr Cymru and has appeared in numerous highly acclaimed productions with the company over the past seven years. Other credits include seasons at the Torch Theatre in Milford Haven, Stafford Castle and also a stint in London's West End. On TV Kai has appeared in *Treflan* and *Tipyn o Stad* for S4C, *Casualty* and *Fun at the Funeral Parlour* for the BBC. He has just finished filming a new TV series called *Rocketman* with Robson Green which will appear on BBC1 this autumn.

Designer: Max Jones

Max graduated from the Royal Welsh College of Music and Drama in 2001 with a first class honours in Theatre Design. He was also a winner of the Linbury Biennial Prize for Stage Design in 2001. This is Max's third design for **sgript**cymru, having previously designed *Franco's Bastard* and *past away*. Max has worked with a number of companies in and around Wales such as Clwyd Theatr Cymru and Welsh National Opera, as well as the Young Vic, London. He has also assisted London-based designer Giles Cadle on leading productions such as *His Dark Materials* (Royal National Theatre), *Lulu* (Munich Opera) and more recently *Much Ado About Nothing* (Sheffield Crucible) and *The Hypochondriac* (The Almeida).

Lighting Designer: Jeanine Davies

Jeanine's credits include: *The BFG* (West End); *Cat on a Hot Tin Roof*, (Nottingham, Coventry, Lyceum); *Angels Among the Trees*, *Polygraph*, (Nottingham Playhouse); *Stone City Blue* (Clwyd Theatr Cymru); *Clockwork* (ROH Linbury Studio); *A Christmas Carol* (Derby); *The Broken Heart* (RSC); *Il Re Pastore* (The Classical Opera Company); *Tom's Midnight Garden* (tour/New York); *Gypsy*, *Macbeth*, *Measure for Measure* (Dundee Rep); *Tartuffe*, *Laurel and Hardy* (also Dublin Festival), *Look Back in Anger* (& Bath), *A Madman Sings to the Moon*, *Uncle Varick*, *A View From the Bridge* (& also on No 1 tour) and *Misery Guts* (Edinburgh Lyceum); Pitlochry Season 2005; *Lareigne* and *Uncanny* (X Factor Dance Company); *Almost But Not Quite* (Dancebase) and *Lifeboat* (both Edinburgh Festival 2005); *The Woman Who Cooked her Husband* (tour); *Zlata's Diary*, *Werewolves* (Communicado); *Don Pasquale* (Scottish Opera Go Round); *Ay Carmela!* (Traverse).

Sound Designer: James Williams

Originally from Llanelli but now based in Cardiff, James works variously as a musical director, director and composer/lyricist. As a composer/musical director James has worked for the Torch Theatre Company, Hijinx Theatre, Theatre Royal Plymouth, the Sherman Theatre Company, Carlson Dance Company, Theatr y Byd, Welsh National Opera, Equinox Theatre, the English Shakespeare Company,

Greenwich Theatre, Made in Wales Theatre Company, the Millennium Dome and the National Health Service. He has collaborated with writer Lesley Ross on *Jorindel & the Nightingale*, *The Sheep Chronicles*, *Pick a Ticket* and *The Jolly Folly of Polly the Scottish Trolley Dolly* – a fifteen minute musical. Last summer James worked as directing mentor for the British Council Drama Festival in Kolkata, India.

Movement and Company Director: Stephen Fisher

Originally from the Elephant and Castle, south London, Stephen Fisher graduated with joint honours in English and Drama from the University of Wales, Swansea in the 1980s having performed in many plays and directed Berkoff's *East* to much acclaim. Shortly afterwards he taught in London before returning to co-create the award-winning Volcano Theatre Company. Having toured the UK and Europe he left to follow a freelance career as a director, actor and lecturer. His work has been seen from Australia to Brussels to Carmarthen and beyond. Having directed a radio comedy and an arts documentary for BBC Television he returned to the theatre as the Associate Director of the Sherman Theatre, Cardiff, directing many plays for the company in his four years there, as well as running the Youth and Education Departments. He has chosen to return to freelance work, most recently with Theatr Na n'Og, Clwyd Theatr Cymru, Theatr Genedlaethol Cymru, BBC Wales and of course **sgript**cymru, with whom he is delighted to be working again.

Production Manager: Sarah Cole

Having spent the last 11 years working professionally in Wales, Sarah now works freelance specialising in production and site management both for theatre and outdoor events. Over the last four years she has worked for the Royal Welsh College of Music and Drama, Clear Channel Entertainment, SJM, Wales Theatre Company, Freshwater UK, Cardiff County Council, **sgript**cymru and the Wales Millennium Centre. Sarah is the Chair of the Theatr Iolo Board and a member of the Stonewall Cymru Council.

Company Stage Manager: Richard Balshaw

Since graduating from the Royal Welsh College of Music and Drama in 1999, Richard has worked for many theatre, television and event companies in the UK and abroad. In 2004, Richard was touring with Riverdance Avoca Company in Europe and Scandinavia as part of the production team. Recently, he has been working with BBC Wales, Rhythm of Life and Production 78 Limited on various outdoor events, and broadcasts all over the UK. *Life of Ryan... and Ronnie* will be Richard's second production with **sgript**cymru, and he is looking forward to being part of a fantastic company again.

Technical Stage Manager: Jane Lalljee

Jane was born in Birmingham and gained a degree in English and History from De Montfort University, Leicester. She moved to Cardiff in 1993 to study an Advanced Diploma Course in Stage Management at the Royal Welsh College of Music and Drama. She has been based in Wales ever since and has worked with various companies including Theatr Iolo, Gwent Theatre, Spectacle, Theatre Centre and Hijinx. Last year, she worked as Company Stage Manager with Clwyd Theatr Cymru on a mid-scale Welsh tour. Most recently, she has been working with The Sherman Theatre in Cardiff on their Under 5s Christmas Tour and she has just completed a national tour with Hijinx. This is her first show with **sgript**cymru.

Costume Supervisor: Sue Jackson

Since graduating in theatre design from the Royal Welsh College of Music and Drama, Sue has worked with many stage companies including Theatr Na n'Og, Gwent Theatre, The Sherman, Spectacle and Caerphilly Youth Theatre. She has also worked as a costume supervisor and stylist on a range of television and feature film productions. Recently, Sue spent two seasons touring as head of wardrobe with the English Touring Opera. This is Sue's second job with **sgript**cymru, having been costume supervisor on *AMDANI!* in 2003.

Assistant Director: Arwel Gruffydd

Arwel trained at Webber Douglas Academy. Earlier this year he appeared in *Cofio Cyfnod: Cofio Graham* – a tribute to the late Graham Laker at the Eryri National Eisteddfod. He was winner of the D. M. Davies Award 2002 for writing, directing and producing a short film, *Cyn Elo'r Haul*. He has also directed *Y Consuriwr*, a short film for Opus Television and he has written and co-produced another short, *Amser Chwarae/Playtime*.

Arwel has been a professional actor for 18 years and his acting credits for **sgript**cymru include *Diwrnod Dwynwen* and *Drws Arall i'r Coed*.

LIFE OF RYAN... AND RONNIE

by **MEIC POVEY**

Characters:

        RYAN

        RONNIE

House lights go down. Over the crackly tannoy, a male-voice choir sings:

'We'll keep a welcome in the hillsides...!
We'll keep a welcome in the vales...!'

VOICE OVER
TANNOY: Ladies and gentlemen...! Please put your hands together ... for Ryan and Ronnie!

Applause.

Ronnie *comes bouncing on in a black DJ to the intro of 'Did You Ever See'.*

RONNIE: 'Do you know my sister Anna
She do play the grand piana
She do also play the fiddle
Up the sides...'

He pauses for a second as he realises he's on his own.

RONNIE: '...and down the middle
Did you ever see
Did you ever see ...!'

He stops completely.

RONNIE: Hold on, Defi John!

The music stops.

RONNIE: He was here a minute ago – honest! Drum roll, Benny?

Drum roll.

RONNIE: Mr Ryan Davies, ladies and gentlemen!

*End of drum roll. No **Ryan Davies**.*

RONNIE: Ryan, you're on, for crying out loud…! (*To audience*) I'm an hotelier at heart. I don't want to be doing this…!

RYAN: (*Voice off; singing*) 'Bread of heaven...!'

RONNIE: Thank God for that!

***Ryan** appears, wearing a white DJ. Cheers and applause.*

RYAN: 'Bread ... of heaven!'

RONNIE: Where the hell have you been…?

RYAN: 'Feed me 'til I want no more! Feed me ... 'til I want no more!'

RONNIE: Are you listening?

RYAN: Friends…! Romans...! And all living creatures east of Pontlottyn!

RONNIE: Oi! Do you mind? I'm in the middle of a song!

RYAN: Really? Why didn't you say so?

Music strikes up.

RYAN/RONNIE: 'Did you ever see…!
Such a funny thing before… !

Do you know my brother Morgan
He do play the chapel organ…!'

RYAN: You can sing along if you like… !

RYAN/RONNIE:	'He do play the balalaika Without socks, on cold Formica … ! Did you ever see Did you ever see…!'
RYAN:	That's right, Mrs Protheroe! Full throttle!
RYAN/RONNIE:	'Did you ever see Such a funny thing before...! Do you know my cousin Bleddyn…'

The music continues in the background.

RYAN:	Ron, it's interesting you should say that...!
RONNIE:	Is it? What did I say, Ry?
RYAN:	You said ... the very thing ... to the letter almost ... that we've all been waiting to 'ear 'ere tonight!
RONNIE:	Ear 'ere tonight?
RYAN:	That's right, Ron – or Ron, right – whichever way you prefer it; at my age I'm very easy to please!
RONNIE:	At your age, I'm not surprised!
RYAN:	'Ere today, gone tomorrow; take your pick!
RONNIE:	(*Sings*) '... and shovel, I'll be there!'
RYAN/RONNIE:	'I'll be there, I'll be there With my little pick and shovel I'll be there! When the coal comes from the Rhondda With my little pick and shovel I'll be there!'

The music from the 'Did You Ever See' continues in the background.

RONNIE: Did you say pick or prick just then?

RYAN: (*He means it*) That's not funny! My mother wouldn't like it!

RONNIE: Is your mother here?

RYAN: No, she'll be in the other place; keeping the flame alive!

RONNIE: There you go then: out of sight, out of mind!

RYAN: Out of *your* mind! Been in the bar long, have we?

RONNIE: All my life, Davies! It's the only way to go.

RYAN: Rubbish! There are other ways! My way for a start!

RONNIE: (*Sings*) 'I did it my way!'

RYAN: 'Do not go gentle into that good night!'

RONNIE: Shall we carry on with the singing?

RYAN: 'Do you know my cousin Bleddyn ...!'

RYAN/RONNIE:
'He do play the triple telyn … !'

Ryan plays an imaginary harp, whilst humming the opening bars of 'Llwyn Onn'.

RYAN: 'Dum-dum, di-ri dum dum – di-rai-di-di-di-di-dum-dum!'

RYAN/RONNIE: 'He do also play the harpsichord...'

RYAN/RONNIE:
(continued)   But unfortunately the harpsichord has three bloody syllables in it and doesn't scan properly, a word like 'trumpet' would've been better … !
'Did you ever see
Did you ever see …!'

RYAN: All together now…!

RYAN/RONNIE: 'Did you ever see … such a funny thing before!'

Applause. Music continues. They slip into a dance/tap routine.

RONNIE: Pa nosweth yw hi, Ry? Ry, what night is it? Where the hell we playing?

RYAN: Ron – I'm glad you asked me that! It's every night of the week for the rest of our lives, gw'boi!

RONNIE: The rest of our lives!!? That's … that's twenty-three years! Can't we stop?

RYAN: Stop? We can't stop, boi bach! If we stop, the wheels might come off!

RONNIE: We've got wheels? Good grief!

RYAN: We're going to need them; we've a long way to go!

*They carry on with the dance/tap routine, **Ryan** doggedly so, **Ronnie** flagging by the second. **Ryan**, in a series of twirls, exits. **Ronnie** carries on for a few more seconds, slowing down gradually, like an old gramophone record. He comes to a complete stop – and stands there, exhausted.*

RONNIE: He *was* here a minute ago – honest.

Light change. Song over tannoy – Tony and Aloma's 'Mae gen i Gariad'.

Ronnie 'relaxing' (i.e. drink in hand). Ryan appears, in black DJ now, carrying the model of a ship made of silver paper.

RONNIE: What in the name of Christ is that...?

'Christ' is a bit strong for Ryan. He smiles nervously. Ronnie is amused. Ryan thrusts the ship forward for Ronnie to see.

RYAN: It's ... my lucky mascot.

RONNIE: It's a pile of silver paper.

RYAN: No, no – it's a ship. Tramp called Bobbie Burns gave it to me when I was a small boy.

RONNIE: Gave you the ship as well, did he? Boom, boom!

RYAN: He had nothing in the world, yet he made this for me. Genius with his hands, see. Collected bits of silver paper, religiously.

RONNIE: Travelling preacher, was he?

RYAN: Knight of the road!

RONNIE: One for the road – yes, please!

They both smile.

RONNIE: What's it really meant to be?

RYAN: Told you – it's a ship. It's ... going places. On a long journey, hopefully.

RONNIE: We're all on one of those, bach.

RYAN:	I've christened it 'Destiny'!

RONNIE:	(*Ironic*) I like that. Subtle.

RYAN:	(*Softly*) 'Somewhere ... over the rainbow, Way up high...'

*Momentarily, **Ryan** drifts off, lost in a world of magical ships and imaginary journeys. **Ronnie** considers him purposefully.*

RONNIE:	What have I done?

*The sound from the tannoy swells up. Loud applause followed by the expectant buzz of a large audience. **Ronnie** becomes a little tense.*

RYAN:	Nervous?

RONNIE:	Who wouldn't be, in Bala. Shag sheep, don't they?

RYAN:	Only when the visitors aren't looking ... apparently.

***Ronnie** chuckles spontaneously but the smile soon fades.*

RONNIE:	I was happy reading the news. (*He momentarily becomes a solemn newsreader, with a perfect BBC accent*) 'Good evening, the death toll at Aberfan has risen to one hundred and sixteen.'

RYAN:	I was happy teaching!

RONNIE:	No offence, but I'm not here out of choice, understand? I could've gone on to other things; could've carried on in my chosen profession...

RYAN:	(*Appropriate accent*) I could've been a contender!

RONNIE:	Trained, see?
RYAN:	(*A bit incredulous*) Cardiff College of Music and Drama.
RONNIE:	Still trained! (*But he concedes the point*) After a fashion. On top of that, I was born into a show-business family!
RYAN:	Do they have those in Wales? And there's me thinking we were all happy amateurs!
RONNIE:	Look, my father was treading the boards long before I even saw the light of day!
RYAN:	Wash boards, was it?
RONNIE:	Very big, he was.
RYAN:	Really?
RONNIE:	Very big indeed, way back then.
RYAN:	(*After appropriate pause*) Huge in south Carmarthenshire anyway...
RYAN:	(*Laughs*) We could use that!
RONNIE:	You taking the mickey?
RYAN:	Perfect timing, Ron!
RONNIE:	Told you, I'm trained. Now, I have to start all over again!
RYAN:	I'm trained too!
RONNIE:	One year at Central? Do me a favour!

RYAN: Don't mock, that's all my mother would allow!

RONNIE: (*Occupied*) All over again ...

RYAN: 'To begin at the beginning. It is spring, moonless night in the small town...'

RONNIE: In a land that time forgot. Two million people, living in caves and Trecco Bay.

RYAN: Four million sheep…!

RONNIE: And not a decent joke between them.

RYAN: When lo and behold, out of the North Walian mist there came a prophet; a saviour, no less...!

RONNIE: Who said unto the television people at the BBC...

RYAN: The Broken Biscuit Company!

RONNIE: He did say…!

RYAN: (*Very exaggerated North Walian accent*) Let there be professionalism!

RONNIE: (*Very exaggerated 'twp' South Walian accent*) Wassat 'en, love?

RYAN: (*North Walian*) I can offer you a two-year contract, and I won't take no for an answer!

RONNIE: I'm happy reading the news!

RYAN: (*North Walian*) Happiness! You silly boy! What's happiness got to do with anything?

RONNIE: We're not compatible!

RYAN: (*North Walian*) That's a big word for a West Walian!

RONNIE: I know more than him! I was down the billiard hall when he was still playing the organ at Moriah; still stuck in the sour soil of the Black Mountain.

RYAN: (*Song*) 'Tros y Mynydd Du i Rydaman!'

RONNIE: I was *drinking* when he was still deciding whether to put sugar in his tea!

RYAN: (*Appropriate accent*) Lemonade, in a doirty glass, I *hope*? 'Hope'! Bob Hope, he said that. Geddit?

RONNIE: I'm supposed to team up with *that*!?

RYAN: (*North Walian*) Team up, and go out on a mission, my friend!

RONNIE: You will go amongst the cave-dwellers, and you will entertain them in the vernacular tongue!

RYAN: (*North Walian*) You will then switch to the Saxon, and entertain the Treccoites!

RONNIE/RYAN: Laughter, after all, is the same in both languages!

The expectant buzz of the audience swells up again.

RONNIE: So is pain – and fear.

Light change.

RYAN: (*American*) Let's sock it to 'em, buddy!

Ryan, relishing the challenge, exits.

RONNIE: The fear, of knowing you'll die a thousand deaths, once you're out there; trying to be funny. Please tell me you feel the same!

RYAN: (*Voice*) Funny! You abandoned that particular concept long ago, boi bach! Only jokin'!

RONNIE: The pain, of knowing that everybody else in the whole wide world is having a ball. Don't you ever wish you'd rather be in the bar, and not on stage?

RYAN: (*Voice*) Not on stage? Are you mad?

RONNIE: There are millions of people out there you know? All with lives and little routines...

RYAN: (*Voice*) Please, God – let my Charlie Chaplin impersonation be a good one, and I'll never take the word of the Lord in vain again!

RONNIE: Fetching kids from school; emptying bins; clipping toenails by the fire ...

RYAN: (*Voice*)
'The Lord is my shepherd – I shall not want more pie!'
'Oh, I'm getting married in the morning…!
Ding dong the bells are gonna chime…!'

RONNIE: (*Still trying to conduct a normal conversation*) My old man...

RYAN: (*Voice*)
'Said follow the van!
And don't dilly-dally on the way...!'

RONNIE:	He said ...
RYAN:	(*Voice – A fire and brimstone preacher now*) He restoreth my soul...! He leadeth me into the path of Mary, Mountain Terrace, popularly known as 'Mary go-round', for his name's sake...!
RONNIE:	He said to me, once...!
RYAN:	(*Voice*) 'Hen fenyw fach Cydweli! Yn gwerthu losin du...!'
RONNIE:	'Ron, if ever you get a word in edgeways, take it!'

*Lights change. Intro-style music. Spotlight picks up **Ryan**'s entrance, made up as a brassy blond – wig, full make-up, the lot. Very loud applause and cheers greets his appearance.*

RYAN:	(*Bursting into song – 'Just One Cornetto'*) 'Ys – tal – y – fera! Give it to me! Behind the bike shed! For one and three!'
RONNIE:	Gladys, how lovely to see you! Where have you been of late?
RYAN:	(*Very 'Valleys'*) 'Where have you been of late?' Where have you been of late! Where have *you* been? What we doin' all of a sudden? Mr Shakespeare's in town, is he?

***Ronnie** giggles; an obvious corpse. **Ryan**'s gone off script but **Ronnie** doesn't mind.*

RONNIE:	That's very funny, Ryan! I mean 'Gladys'...!

A mistake. Both corpse.

RYAN: (*Gladys*) You goin' to ask me something, or do I have to talk to the band?

RONNIE: (*'Act'*) Tell me, Gladys...!

RYAN: (*Gladys*) Yes, young man? (*Turns to audience*) He's a nice boy, innee...!

RONNIE: Tell me...

RYAN: (*Gladys; very flirty*) I'll tell you all; I surrender; I'm all yours!

RONNIE: Tell me about your trip to north Wales...

RYAN: (*Gladys*) My trip to see the transvestiture? Don't ask!

RONNIE: Surely you mean the *in*vestiture?

RYAN: (*Gladys*) You call it what you like, bach – I know what I mean! Like the frock? Yes...! The *trans*vestiture! They were all there at C'narfyn, the great and the good of Wales – some even came from Prestatyn!

RONNIE: That's a cheap laugh!

RYAN: (*Gladys*) Ever been to Prestatyn?

RYAN/RONNIE: Boom, boom!

RONNIE: Did you see Prince Charles?

RYAN: (*Gladys*) Did I see Prince Charles...?! (*He pauses*) You did ask me that just now, didn't yew?

RONNIE: No, it's an echo.

Ronnie corpses as he says the line. It's an obvious ad-lib.

RYAN: (*Gladys*) Ann Echo? I didn't know she was coming tonight!

RONNIE: Could we get back to Caernarfon, please? Did you get to see Prince Charles at all?

RYAN: (*Gladys*) Oh, the ears on that boy! Puts Jumbo the elephant to shame he does; a bit of northerly down the Menai Straits and he'd be off! No, let's be serious for a minute. I went there in my Hillman Imp...

RONNIE: Is that what you drive?

RYAN: (*Gladys*) It doesn't drive itself, I'll tell you for nothing!

RONNIE: So you went up to north Wales in your Hillman Imp – then what?

RYAN: (*Gladys*) That was the plan, cariad: me, Blodwen, Meirwen and Siân. But we got lost; yes, got lost; and do you know why? Do you know anything?

RONNIE: Paris is the capital of France!

RYAN: (*Gladys*) This boy's a genie…!

RONNIE: Don't you mean 'genius'?

RYAN: (*Gladys*) Ave a rub; see what you think!

RONNIE: Why did you get lost, Gladys?

RYAN:	(*Gladys*) Ten miles out of Ponty, all the signs were painted green!
RONNIE:	Never!
RYAN:	(*Gladys*) Never in Europe, gw'boi, but they were! 'How Green Was My Valet', myn yffarn i!

Ronnie laughs at this unexpected ad-lib.

RYAN:	(*Gladys*) They should be laughing by *there* now! (*audience*)
RONNIE:	You mean 'How Green Was My *Valley*', don't you?
RYAN:	(*Gladys*) Don't know about yours, petal, but mine was as black as the ace of spades!

Ronnie giggles.

RYAN:	(*Himself*) He's off again!
RONNIE:	Shall we move on?
RYAN:	(*Gladys*) Got your own car? The Hillman's full!

Loud laughter; applause; music. Light change. **Ronnie** *is euphoric, pouring himself drinks, chain-smoking, fiddling with bits of paper, scribbling.* **Ryan** *is stern; thoughtful.*

RYAN:	Not so clever now, eh?
RONNIE:	Keep the ad-libs! Bloody funny!
RYAN:	Which ones?
RONNIE:	Which ones?

RYAN:	Which ones! Ann Echo still here, is she?
RONNIE:	That one! Bloody funny!
RYAN:	What about the corpse?
RONNIE:	What about it?
RYAN:	That was no ad-lib...
RONNIE:	That was my wife! Boom, boom!
RYAN:	It was a mistake, boi bach...
RONNIE:	They laughed!
RYAN:	No, we laughed; we lost control.
RONNIE:	'Ann Echo' was funny, Ry!
RYAN:	I made it funny!
RONNIE:	Does it matter who made it?
RYAN:	Not if the both of us can do it; both of us have to be able to take them on! Ann Echo? I didn't know she was coming tonight? Boom, boom! You could've made it funnier, but no, you chose the easy option and scurried back to the safety of the script...
RONNIE:	We'd still be out there if I hadn't!
RYAN:	You could've picked it up, Ron! There was another laugh goin' begging!
RONNIE:	Really?

RYAN:	Yes, really! Another laugh, a lost opportunity. Ann Echo? I didn't know she was coming tonight! Yes, she phoned earlier and I got her a comp!
RONNIE:	That's ... funny?
RYAN:	It's half way there. But to be really funny ... Are you listening to this?
RONNIE:	Why, is it important?
RYAN:	It's number one, page one...
RONNIE:	In the Ryan Davies bestseller, *Comedy for One!*
RYAN:	To be really funny, Ron...
RONNIE:	Yes, master?
RYAN:	We two shouldn't be having fun!
RONNIE:	(*Stunned*) Well a jiw jiw!

Lights change. **Ryan** *goes off.*

RONNIE:	No fun? Sunday school trip to Porthcawl; sea and candy floss; mustn't enjoy because of the religious element. I think we might be on a bit of a collision course here; only time will tell. It's not all bad, I suppose: gleaming white Jaguar apiece; the world our oyster; no challenge too difficult. But no fun? I'd rather end it all now. (*He pauses to reflect*) Hotelier at heart, see? Like my dad before me. Publican with a bit of entertaining on the side. I could make a go of it.

Ryan *comes on, changes from Gladys to black DJ.*

RYAN:	So...! Could you please tell the court how much you owe, Mr Williams?
RONNIE:	Is this a sketch?
RYAN:	It's life.
RONNIE:	(*Proudly*) Twenty-eight grand. If you must fall on your arse, fall big I say.
RYAN:	I didn't realise comedians were so pricey!
RONNIE:	Ken Dodd at Ronnie's! Long way from Cefneithin Welfare Hall I can tell you!
RYAN:	Cabaret room at Cerrigydrudion, eh? Do the Tibetans like cabaret?
RONNIE:	Materials! Didn't realise wood was so expensive!
RYAN:	Are we talking about Ken Dodd again?
RONNIE:	Not to mention the workers...
RYAN:	The workers?
RONNIE:	I told you not to mention them.
RYAN/RONNIE:	Boom, boom!
RONNIE:	Even mates don't work for peanuts.
RYAN:	Is that your defence?
RONNIE:	No, it's an extremely large vodka and tonic.

RYAN: In a pint glass...

RONNIE: There's a perfectly reasonable explanation!

RYAN: I'm all ears.

RONNIE: Have a word with Noddy.

Spontaneously, they both giggle.

RYAN: Steady, cariad...!

They consider each other, fondly.

RONNIE: Why did it all have to end...!

RYAN: It was you, remember...?

RONNIE: Shit, aye! It's all coming back to me!

Shared laughter.

RYAN: Won't you tell the court about the pint glass, Mr Williams?

RONNIE: It's nothing. It's just a prop.

RYAN: A crutch? This is very interesting, m'lud!

RONNIE: It's ... an accessory! It keeps me on my toes!

RYAN: It keeps him in the bar, ladies and gentlemen of the jury!

RONNIE: Gives me that extra bite! Look in the mirror why don't you!

RYAN:	(*Himself*) What do you mean?
RONNIE:	Would you mind explaining to the court what your mother had to say when you left the safety of state employment, Mr Davies!
RYAN:	My mother's got nothing to do with it!
RONNIE:	The drink's got nothing to do with it!
RYAN:	You could live without the drink?
RONNIE:	Oh, yes! I could ... (*He momentarily falters*) ... definitely live without the drink. Could *you* live without...?
RYAN:	(*Interrupts him*) I'm at a loss as to what my learned friend is trying to prove, m'lud!
RONNIE:	(*Himself*) Oh, bugger this! I'm simply trying to say that everybody has their own fucking cross to bear! Who are you – God!?
RYAN:	Could we move on, please? Who started this nonsense anyway?
RONNIE:	*This* nonsense? It was you, remember?
RYAN:	(*Reflects*) Aye, it was too. It's all coming back to me...

Shared smile as the lights fade and music plays.

When the lights come up again, and as the music gradually fades, we find **Ronnie** *scribbling, drinking, smoking.* **Ryan***, like a coiled spring, pacing up and down, puffing on an absolute monster of a cigar, pausing intermittently to admire his reflection.*

RYAN: By God, Davies, but you're beautiful!

He puffs on his cigar; he has a severe coughing bout; he fights for his breath; he sticks an asthma pump in his mouth and gives himself a blast.

RYAN: Keep goin', bach!

He breathes deeply; he is OK again. **Ronnie** *picks up a dictaphone.*

RYAN: Right, Williams…! Here's the plan of attack!

RONNIE: (*Into dictaphone*) Heart-attack, twenty-second April, seventy-seven...

RYAN: After a full morning's rehearsal, we hit the road for Tibet mid-afternoon!

RONNIE: (*Dictaphone*) Groeslon Village Hall. Postmistress came in.

RYAN: And what a road!

RONNIE: Just the solitary name, like Twiggy or Topol.

RYAN: Two hundred miles of wilderness and not a soul in sight!

RONNIE: (*Dictaphone*) Where were you when Kennedy was shot?

RYAN: Pwllheli Yacht Club! Dot of eight!

RONNIE: (*Dictaphone*) When Armstrong walked the moon...

RYAN: A willing audience for me please; a vodka tonic for Ron!

RONNIE: Make that a large one!

RYAN: Sound-check; song-check; script-check!

RONNIE: Go on then: just the one more!

RYAN: Nine o'clock, hit the stage!

RONNIE: The barmaid's name is Betty; she's a big fan!

RYAN: Wrap up at eleven; mad dash to Anglesey; late night cabaret at Menai Bridge!

RONNIE: The barmaid's name is Glenys! Haia, love, make mine a triple!

RYAN: Get up at the crack of dawn! (*Annoyed*) Hang about!

RONNIE: God, is that the time!

RYAN: Fifty-seven minutes! An hour, almost! Wasted! Gone, never to be retrieved!

RONNIE: Can we stop at Dinas Mawddwy on the way; see Danny, Chris and all the boys?

RYAN: Another two hours! It's killing me!

RONNIE: Have a drink, and a bit of a sing-song! 'Bing bong a bing bong be!'

RYAN/RONNIE: 'Bing bong a bing bong be!'

RYAN: Cardiff! Half-eight at the latest! Sound-check; song-check; script-check!

RONNIE: Snow-check; singe-chick; skid-neck! Oh, sugar!

RYAN: Ha! Not so chirpy now, folks!

*Lights change. Music: intro into chat-show. During the light change, **Ryan**
goes off. **Ronnie** picks up a hand-held microphone.*

RONNIE: Good evening, ladies and gentlemen...! And welcome
to *Late Call*. My name is Ronnie Williams, and my very
special guest this week is a star of stage, screen and the
South Wales Echo!

Laughter.

RYAN: (*Voice*) I'm very big down under too!

Laughter.

RONNIE: Of course, there's no need for surnames; everybody
knows, don't they? Please give a warm, Broadway welcome
– that's Broadway, Splott by the way, madam – or ... (*Posh*)
... 'Sploe' as they say locally...

RYAN: (*Voice*) Get on with it!

RONNIE: Ryan, ladies and gentlemen!

*Music. Applause. **Ryan** bounces on.*

RONNIE: Ryan, welcome...!

RYAN: Shw'mai, Ron!

RONNIE: So then ... exciting times?

RYAN: (*Gladys*) If you think 'avin Ted Heath as Prime Minister
is exciting you've got a problem, boi bach! I'd rather 'ave
a night out with my ex-husband!

RONNIE:	What's he doing these days?
RYAN:	(*Gladys*) Not much – they buried him last spring!
RONNIE:	Is this in the script?
RYAN:	(*Himself now*) No, but I've heard you need all the laughs you can get!
RONNIE:	Seriously though...
RONNIE/RYAN:	And comedy is a sad and serious business – boom, boom!
RONNIE:	Seriously – you've had a big breakdown recently, haven't you ... um ... I mean breakthrough!
RYAN:	One step at a time, Williams, one step at a time! (*To chat-show audience*) He didn't even get past the auditions!
RONNIE:	*Under Milk Wood*, Second Voice, you must be over the moon?
RYAN:	Over the moon, under milk wood indeed, Ron! Over and under, or up and under as we used to say in Glanaman – or maybe that's just Eddie Wearing. It's confusing, whichever way you look at it...
RONNIE:	But exciting for you personally? Tell me about Burton...
RYAN:	Small, pock-marked thespian from Pontrhydyfen!
RONNIE:	You can't say that on national television!
RYAN:	Of course not; and I don't mean it, not for one second. He's a great star, one of the few genuine Hollywood stars remaining. It's a great privilege...

RONNIE:	Must be.
RYAN:	Yes, for him now! No, no, seriously ... it's a dream; the chance of a lifetime. (*Burtonesque*) 'To begin at the beginning: it is spring, moonless night in the small town ...'
RONNIE:	That's *First* Voice, isn't it?
RYAN:	(*Valleys*) Aye butt, made a bit of a mistake there, that Sinclair producer fellow.
RONNIE:	Seriously...
RYAN:	Seriously, Ron? He said to me; I asked him: 'I understand you've been to see your lawyer today, Mr Burton ... Richard...'
RONNIE:	Is that his proper name – Mr Burton Richard?
RYAN:	(*Burton*) That's correct, Ryan. Come and have a drink. (*Himself*) Went too! He told me how much divorcing Liz was likely to cost him. Met her!
RONNIE:	(*To audience*) She wouldn't recognise him again if he fell into her vodka, head first!
RYAN:	I was with them for two hours!
RONNIE:	Drinking with the chauffeur, while they were upstairs having it off.
RYAN:	I was with the stars, while you were still doing blinkin' quiz shows!
RONNIE:	*Chat* shows, please.

False laughter from both.

RYAN: Tell me, Ron – what did Burton have to say when you and the film crew came down to Fishguard? (*American*) I'm sure the audience would love to know!

RONNIE: Hell, mun – you know what he said! You were there!

RYAN: Can you say 'hell' on national television?

RONNIE: He said...!

RYAN: Do the voice! Do the voice, Ron. He's a trained actor you know!

RONNIE: Don't patronise me!

RYAN: He said that? Bloody cheek!

Ronnie *chuckles spontaneously.*

RONNIE: (*Burtonesque*) Shw'mai, Ronnie. Dda cwrdd â ti. I've heard so much about you.

RYAN: Not *you*!

RONNIE: (*Shares it with 'audience'*) So easy to get him going!

RYAN: What did he say about *me*! (*To 'audience'*) This is the honest truth, aye!

RONNIE: (*Burton*) Ryan here is a major talent, but he should get out. Artistically, on a world stage, Wales is worthy but irrelevant...

RYAN: He said that about me? That's Richard Burton, Ron!

RONNIE: You know he did! You were there! Fucking hell...!

RYAN: A major talent, folks!

RONNIE: (*Exhausted*) Fucking hell, Ry ... what's the matter with you?

They both remember that they're in a TV studio with a live audience.

RYAN: Um ... I think we might have to go again, bach.

RONNIE: I think you're right. (*To invisible floor manager*) OK, Harold...

Ronnie drops the mic to one side. Light change, to reflect studio house-lights coming on. Both relax and loiter in the way people do when waiting for things to happen. Ronnie lights a cigarette. Their conversation is totally normal; they are themselves. Ryan, especially, for once is not 'performing' at all.

RONNIE: How's it really going?

RYAN: I've aged sixty years. So much hanging about. Telly's not in it. One take after another.

RONNIE: Good, innit? You make a mess of it, you start all over again – and you don't get to see the white of their eyes.

RYAN: That's sloppy though, Ron.

RONNIE: It's practical.

RYAN: It's the end of civilisation as we know it. Why can't it be right, first time?

RONNIE: If there's a hair in the gate, there's a hair in the gate. What's a man to do...?

RYAN: Make sure it's not there in the first place.

Pause.

RYAN: People gawping. They stand there for hours, watching
             nothing happening. I can't fathom it; where's the enjoy-
             ment in that? I say, I say, I say – my dog hasn't got a
             nose; really, how does he smell?; terrible. Boom, boom.
             A funny gag. It's tangible. How do you connect when
             nothing's happening?

RONNIE: Harder once you're older.

RYAN: I'm thirty-five, you moron.

RONNIE: Interviewed Des O'Connor the other day. Very chirpy.
             Lovely skin. Wanted to kill the bastard. Did Anita Harris,
             same day. Could give her one.

RYAN: The lack of reality is amazing. Then, when it does go right,
             people congratulate you as if you've just conquered
             Everest.

RONNIE: Aye. You were wonderful, darling!

RYAN: (*Absently*) Thanks. I'm glad mam's not down, witnessing
             the squandering of my talents.

RONNIE: Don't worry, we'll have a nice drink after.

RYAN: Drink? You don't know you're born. Richard puts it on
             his cornflakes in the morning. How can he do that?

RONNIE: What's wrong with a glass? No style. Oh! I see. Yes,
             that's disgusting. Terrible. Had a drink in Cross Hands
             on the way back. I was standing at the bar and this

30

RONNIE: (continued)	bloke came up to me and said: 'Don't I know you?' And I said: 'I'm just having one for the road.' But he didn't want to hear, he only wanted me to tell him where he'd seen me before. 'I know!' he said – 'you used to be Ronnie Williams.' And I said: 'Aye, that's right, and now I'm fucking Mary Whitehouse!' and walked out.

Long pause.

RYAN:	Went into a north Wales chapel, once. As me, right? Ryan Davies, citizen.
RONNIE:	Rare appearance.
RYAN:	The minister, he made a point of commenting on the fact that I was there; that such a familiar face had chosen his chapel to worship in. At least, that's what I thought he was saying. But then, he went on to preach against the very idea of entertainment...
RONNIE:	Never.
RYAN:	Never in Europe gw'boi, but it's true. Calling it wicked, and evil, and the devil's work. My belief in God strengthened twelve-fold that day...
RONNIE:	Really? As much as that...?
RYAN:	Conversely, my disappointment in man diminished by the same degree...
RONNIE:	Took quite a knock myself in Cross Hands.
RYAN:	Couldn't do anything there and then, obviously; couldn't be contrary in the house of worship. But had I been given five minutes with that minister – him sitting, me doing a

RYAN:	turn – he would've quickly seen the error of his ways.
(continued)	Everyone's there to be cracked, Ron. I've even cracked mam on one or two occasions. Let me misquote Dylan for a minute: 'Praise the Lord, we are a "humorous" nation.' And that's right, isn't it? All I'm saying is this: if you think what I do and say is funny, just laugh, and I promise not to ask you why...

| RONNIE: | What the fuck are you on about, Ry? (*To invisible floor manager*) OK Harold? (*Microphone up*) Right, let's pick it up! |

*Without missing a beat, **Ryan** drops 'citizen' and adopts 'entertainer.'*

| RYAN: | He said that about me? That's Richard Burton, Ron! |

*He hasn't given an inch. For a second, **Ronnie** thinks about resisting but then relents.*

| RONNIE: | That's right, Ry! And if King Richard said it, it must be spot on! |

| RYAN: | (*'Playing' to the audience*) Would you mind repeating it one more time for the benefit of the hard of hearing? |

Laughter.

| RONNIE: | He said...! |

| RYAN: | (*Finishing the quote*) Ryan Davies is a man of talent! Wales is worthy but the world awaits! Furthermore...! |

| RONNIE: | I'm sorry, I'll have to stop you there, we've run out of time! |

| RYAN: | (*With a forced smile*) You ba ... ritone! |

Laughter.

RONNIE: Of course, no appearance by Ryan would be complete without a song, ladies and gentlemen...!

RYAN: 'You are my sunshine...!'

RONNIE: 'My only sunshine...!'

RYAN/RONNIE: 'You make me happy, when skies are grey,
You'll never know dear, how much I love you,
Please don't take my sunshine away...!'

Applause. They regard each other fondly.

RONNIE: Why did it all have to end?

RYAN: Death and income tax, old friend; death and income tax.

Lights change. Over the tannoy, The Hennessys:

*'I'm Cardiff born, I'm Cardiff bred,
And when I dies I'll be Cardiff dead.
They'll build a little plot in Splott
In memory of me.'*

Ronnie *reading the* Guardian *newspaper (circa early 1970s).* **Ryan** *reading from a printed copy of the play* The Sunshine Boys.

RYAN: (*American*) We got back to the dressing room, he took off his make-up, put his clothes on and said to me:

Ronnie *throws him a look.*

RYAN: *Sunshine Boys*, New Theatre...

RONNIE: Two comedians, who hate each other's guts. Yes, I know.
                You've told me.

RYAN: Bill Owen's playing Al Lewis!

RONNIE: Who the hell's Bill Owen when he's out? I could've played
                that. Thanks for the mensh.

RYAN: (*American*) I could've been a contender! *Last of the
                Summer Wine*; new sitcom?

RONNIE: (*Quoting from the newspaper*) 'Sloeblack, slow, black,
                crow-black, cockle-boat bobbing nightmare.' Film review,
                Guardian. Wanna read?

Ryan ignores this. Resumes reading play.

RYAN: (*American*) He said to me:

RONNIE: They're going to premiere in Venice, with Italian subtitles.
                Helpful.

RYAN: (*American*) He said:

RONNIE: Should've stuck with me, kiddo. Poke your finger in the
                fire and what happens? Bloody hell, that's hot!

Ronnie puts the paper aside and picks up a script.

RYAN: (*American*) Willie, if it's all the same to you, I'm retiring.

RONNIE: (*Act*) Good evening, ladies and gentlemen, it's lovely to
                be back here in Machynlleth once again.

RYAN: (*American*) What do you mean, retiring? It's not even
                nine o'clock. Let's have something to eat.

RONNIE:	(*Act*) Isn't it, Ryan?

RYAN:	(*American*) I'm not retiring for the night, I'm retiring for what's left of my life.

RONNIE:	Eh! That's not it.

RYAN:	What's left of my life...

RONNIE:	(*Act*) It's lovely to be back here in Machynlleth once again ... isn't it, Ryan?

Ronnie waits impatiently while *Ryan* puts on a pair of round, national health spectacles and pulls a bowler hat half way down over his ears.

RONNIE:	When can I expect an answer – now, or this time next year?

RYAN:	(*In character*) Padyn?! (*Pardon*)

RONNIE:	Is that what you're going to say tonight? Stop pissing about!

RYAN:	(*Act*) Yes, Ron, it certainly is...!

RONNIE:	Thank you! (*Act*) It's lovely to be back here in Machynlleth once again, isn't it, Ryan?

RYAN:	(*Act*) Yes, Ron, it certainly is...!

RONNIE:	And it is, isn't it? Don't you feel you know them all personally in a place like this?

RYAN:	I do know them all personally! Alright, love? Round the back, after the show?

RONNIE: That's cheap.

RYAN: Come round the back after the show...

RONNIE: ... and I'll show you cheap.

RYAN: Boom, boom!

Ronnie sighs heavily. Ryan takes off the hat and glasses. Absent-mindedly, certainly not intentionally, Ronnie flicks his ash over Ryan's silver ship; his lucky mascot. Ryan's face tightens as he picks up the ship and carefully dusts it down.

RONNIE: Sorry – didn't realise it was there.

RYAN: (*Quiet passion*) You leave my ship alone, you bastard.

A raised eyebrow from Ronnie; Ryan doesn't often swear.

RYAN: Should he return; if he comes knocking on my door, I want to be able to hand it back in pristine condition. 'Didn't work out, Bobbie. I did my utmost, gave it my best shot, but there you go. Long journey, cut short. Thanks anyway.'

Light change, favouring Ronnie.

RONNIE: I've met 'em all: Cliff Richard; Marty Wilde; Helen Shapiro...! Even met that Ryan Davies bloke once. We were doing panto ... (*He chuckles*) See, I'm laughing already! Dick Whittington; the cat, or something. He had a wig and a hat, and he put the hat on and the wig on top of it. Hysterical. Bloody hysterical!

Pause.

RONNIE: I was doing this piece; I was playing a psychiatric patient. After rehearsal, I ran out of the room crying. Went down the bridge at Cardigan to have a think. River looked nice. Too busy though...

*The light fades on **Ronnie**. Over the tannoy, Margaret Williams singing:*

'Nico annwyl ei di drosta i
Ar negas fach i Gymru lân...'

*Light change. **Ryan** and **Ronnie** are together. **Ronnie** is as tense as we've ever seen him.*

RONNIE: Pa nosweth yw hi, Davies? What night is it? Where we playing for God's sake?

RYAN: Every night ... for the rest of our lives.

RONNIE: Really? We need a holiday!

RYAN: A holiday! Rubbish! (*À la Eric Morecambe*) The boy's a fool! We need a new challenge; a bigger stage!

RONNIE: Will a state funeral do you? I think it might be on the cards!

RYAN: That's good! Can we use it?

RONNIE: No, but we could book ourselves a month in the sun!

RYAN: A month! A whole month! Why ... that's ... that's...

RONNIE: Nearly an armful!

Both laugh.

RYAN: That's four weeks, Ron. It's a helluva long time, bach! And once it's gone, we'll never get it back. An opportunity, lost forever.

RONNIE: Is that what you'll tell 'em at the pearly gates? I sat on my arse in Benidorm for a month, but I can make it up to you now? Will God appreciate a Charlie Chaplin impersonation? Think about it; we could have it all: sun, sea, sangria. Water skiing! What do you say?

RYAN: Wouldn't mind having a go at that, actually. It looks difficult.

Light change: end of the pier; garish; tacky; a burst of music, in similar vein. **Ryan** *and* **Ronnie** *slip into song and dance routine.*

RYAN/RONNIE: 'Oh, I do like to be beside the seaside!
                   Oh, I do like to be beside the sea!
                   Oh, I do like to stroll along the prom, prom, prom!
                   When the brass band plays tiddly om pom pom!

                   Oh, just let me be beside the seaside
                   I'd be beside myself with glee
                   There's a lot of girls besides
                   I should like to be beside
                   Beside the seaside, beside the sea!'

Applause.

RYAN: Noswaith dda, foneddigion a boneddigesau – a chroeso! Yes, that's right, Mrs Wigginbottom, that was *Welsh*! And you don't understand Welsh, do you?

RONNIE: (*A touch of irony*) Certainly not in Blackpool!

RYAN: Hey, Ron, I don't think they understand the old vernacular!

38

RONNIE: Vernacular, Ry? Is that rude?

RYAN: In the right light, it can be very rude!

Squeals of suggestive laughter.

RONNIE: (*Aside*) Knicker audience! (*Act*) Excuse me, sir! You can't bring that dog in 'ere – this is a pier!

RYAN: So's this dog!

More over-the-top laughter. **Ryan** *laps it up;* **Ronnie** *grins and bears it.*

RONNIE: Shall I tell you...? What the nipper said to me? You know, when we were last home, three hundred years ago...

RYAN: I remember it well! Found out I had a wife and two children!

Laughter.

RONNIE: Precisely my point! And do you know what one of them said to me? He said...!

RYAN: It's Ronnie Williams, star of stage, screen and Central Pier, Blackpool! I know that man!

RONNIE: He doesn't! That's the problem!

RYAN: Problem? What about all the presents, the big house, the chauffeur-driven limousine?

RONNIE: You speak for yourself!

Laughter.

RONNIE:	He said...! He said to me; we were sitting in front of the telly, Sunday evening; we were sitting there when *Maes a Môr* comes on; the religious programme?
RYAN:	I am familiar with *Maes a Môr*, Ron.
RONNIE:	Well, you would be. Anyway, we're sitting there; it comes up on the telly, and he says, sort of half to himself...
RYAN:	Stage whisper!
RONNIE:	To no–one in particular, but loud enough to be heard; he says: 'Oh, no – Maes a frigging Môr!' Would you like a translation?
RYAN:	He said that?
RONNIE:	'Maes a frigging Môr' – only he did not say 'frigging', ladies and gentlemen!

Laughter.

RYAN:	Getting all the laughs, eh? It must be Christmas!

Laughter.

RONNIE:	My own son! Ten!
RYAN:	That's what Welsh telly does to you I suppose!
RONNIE:	It's not funny.
RYAN:	What did you do?
RONNIE:	I turned around and said; I asked the wife, 'What did he say just then?' I asked him: '*What* did you say?'

RYAN: What's your point?

Laughter.

Ryan *realises that* **Ronnie**'s *wheels are gradually coming off. He is abandoning the 'act' and flirting dangerously with reality.*

RONNIE: My point is this: had I been there for him, these last few years, he wouldn't have dared say it! He might've thought it, he might've thought 'I'm not sitting here watching this frigging rubbish...'

RYAN: Only he did not say 'frigging', ladies and gentlemen!

Laughter.

RONNIE: Let me finish, will you! He'd go to his room, not say it out loud! That's my point. All of which begs the question – where's my authority? What's my role, Ry?

RYAN: 'What's my role, Ry?' I can feel a song coming on!

RONNIE: Aye, there's always a song isn't there; and a bit of a routine!

RYAN: Of course there is! We're in Blackpool! We're on holiday!

RONNIE: Some fucking holiday!

Shocked 'Oh!' reaction from the audience.

RYAN: Um ... shouldn't that be 'frigging', butt?

Few weak laughs as the light fades.

Light change.

RYAN:	Get a grip. We're all homesick. 'Fish would be nice tonight, dear.' Yes, and it would be lovely too. But sometimes, it has to take a back seat. After all...!
RONNIE:	The show must go on!
RYAN:	Onwards and upwards, Ron!
RONNIE:	Roll up, roll up, roll up! Come and marvel at the bearded lady! Let the elephant man frighten the life out of you! Come see the two boyos making absolute twats of themselves!
RYAN:	Don't ... use that word in my presence.
RONNIE:	Boyos?
RYAN:	You are so predictable.
RONNIE:	Ha! Pot? Black?
RYAN:	That word! It makes me ill, to think that such a word has wormed its way into the very fabric of the Welsh nation!

Ronnie roars with laughter at *Ryan*'s pomposity.

RYAN:	And anyway, you're wrong: all I can hear is the laughter.
RONNIE:	All I can hear are the twats. Laughter? Who cares, Davies! Who's going to remember in thirty years' time! A bowl of dust, that's all we'll be!
RYAN:	Remember? Who's going to remember, indeed…! (*He thinks about it*) How old was that woman who wet herself at Cemmaes Road? Could be still alive in thirty years' time, couldn't she?

RONNIE:	But will she *remember*, Ry? Ryan and Ronnie, no, don't tell me, yes, it's all coming back to me now. Ventriloquists, weren't they?
RYAN:	(*Beaten momentarily*) Goggle of gear; goggle of gear. (*But then he is strong again*) Go then, if you must! Go back home; on holiday; I'll carry on alone!
RONNIE:	Oh, yes…! You'd love that…
RYAN:	No choice.
RONNIE:	Love the excuse! Well – just remind yourself what people have said about me before you do anything stupid!
RYAN:	What have they been saying? Nothing nasty, I hope …
RONNIE:	They recognise me for what I am for starters! A vital cog.
RYAN:	Vital cog; bright spark; spanner in the works. Just sayings…
RONNIE:	Graham Jones, he said it, not me.
RYAN:	I know – that milkman from Aberporth. Great bloke.
RONNIE:	*Guardian* newspaper! Talented; respected…
RYAN:	Is that what he said about you? Left out 'lush'…
RONNIE:	(*Quoting*) 'Ryan's a tremendously versatile comedian; yes, he can sing well, dance, tell a good story, give impressions and has shown considerable talents as a straight actor…'

RYAN: Good to see that your capacity to learn lines hasn't deserted you completely, Ronnie.

RONNIE: (*Quoting*) 'Indeed ... he deserves to succeed internationally. But I would miss Ronnie.' Miss Ronnie! You listening to this? 'Ryan seems to me to need a partner, a butt for his humour.' '*Needs*', Davies! That's what the man said! Graham Jones, *Guardian* newspaper! It's not all one-way traffic!

*Light change. **Ronnie** goes off. **Ryan** considers his silver ship; runs a delicate finger over it pensively. He puts his feet up; rests his head back and shuts his eyes.*

Music/song softly in the background:

'Somewhere, over the rainbow
Way up high
There's a land that I heard of
Once in a lullaby', etc.

*During the song, **Ronnie** reappears, smoking a fat cigar. He clocks that Ryan is asleep. He smokes his cigar, reflectively. The following exchanges are 'voices' only.*

RONNIE: (*American*) We're looking to do *Fiddler on the Roof*, Mr Davies – interested?

RYAN: (*Exaggerated South Walian accent*) Intyrested? Intyrested, lovely boy!

'If I were a rich man…!
Yaga daga daga daga daga dum!
All day long I'd bidi bidi bum
If I were a wealthy man...!'

RONNIE:	(*American*) Move closer to Mr Davies, Miss Streisand...?
RYAN:	(*South Walian*) Yes, come closer, Barbra bach, it's shorter than you think!
RONNIE:	(*American*) Tell me – what have you done in England?
RYAN:	(*Himself*) Let me correct you straight away: I'm from Wales, not England!
RONNIE:	(*American*) Sure. Wales, England – I know it. That's a swell name you've got there; it's a good start. We have quite a few of our own as a matter of fact: Ryan O'Neill; Robert Ryan...
RYAN:	Von Ryan's Express!
RONNIE:	(*American*) Great actor; great guy! You a comic, like Benny Hill? You've certainly got the physique!
RYAN:	No, no – Benny Hill's English, I'm Welsh; from Wales. But I'm not a Welsh entertainer; I'm an entertainer who happens to be Welsh.
RONNIE:	(*American*) I understand. Richard Burton came through here once.
RYAN:	I've worked with Richard Burton!
RONNIE:	(*American*) No kidding? Sat right there, where you are now.
RYAN:	Really?
RONNIE:	(*American*) Just done *Virginia Woolf*! Terrific movie! Should've cleaned up at the Oscars, but there you go! Maybe it'll be your turn, some day!

Ryan wakes up and shoots to his feet.

RYAN: And the winner is...!

*He gradually realises he's been dreaming. He stares down at **Ronnie**, almost accusingly; he clocks the cigar.*

RONNIE: Ran out of ciggies. Don't mind, do you?

Over the tannoy, Tony and Aloma sing:

'Pat a Janet ac Elsi a Glen
Galwch i'w gweld nhw yng nghaffi Gaerwen
Anodd yw peidio a cholli eich pen
'Da Pat a Janet ac Elsi a Glen'

Ronnie *picks up the dictaphone.*

RONNIE: (*To the dictaphone*) Bla bla bla ... and the guy says: ''Ere, this isn't chocolate, this is shit!' And Ianto says: 'Aye, that's right, do you want to buy a toothbrush?!'

Ronnie *chuckles to himself; he likes it.*

RYAN: You can't say 'shit'.

RONNIE: Wassat...?

RYAN: You can't say 'shit' on English television.

RONNIE: Kenneth Tynan said 'fuck'!

RYAN: He wasn't meant to! It wasn't planned. Billy Cotton would have us through the door before you could say... (*He lets it go*)

RONNIE:	Shit?

They almost smile – but don't.

RONNIE:	The gag doesn't work without 'shit'.
RYAN:	Don't use the gag.
RONNIE:	It's a good gag! What the hell am I supposed to do?
RYAN:	Whatever it is, you're doing it on purpose.
RONNIE:	I am?
RYAN:	The plumber's here, cariad! Oh, how much is he charging? A hundred pounds. A hundred pounds! That's a bit steep, it's only a ten quid job! Get another plumber!
RONNIE:	What the hell was that?
RYAN:	*Fait accompli.* You know.
RONNIE:	No need to swear!
RYAN:	Don't be afraid of a little English.
RONNIE:	Ah! Now then – hold on, Defi John! You know as well as I do, there's English, and there's:
RYAN:	(*Very Welsh*) 'Who's coat is that jacket?'
RONNIE:	Exactly!
RYAN:	'I'll be there now in a minute!'
RONNIE:	I rest my case!

RYAN:	'If you break a leg, don't come running to me!'
RONNIE:	Will the English have heard of Mr Thomas from Sketty, Ry? Mr Williams from Seven Sisters? Not to mention the lady who wet herself at Cemmaes Road!
RYAN:	The lady who wet herself at Cemmaes Road, Ron?
RONNIE:	I told you not to mention that.
RYAN/RONNIE:	Boom, boom!
RONNIE:	Seriously...
RYAN/RONNIE:	And comedy is a sad and serious business, folks!
RONNIE:	No ... seriously, seriously butt: will they have heard of them; and what about your mam?
RYAN:	You leave my mam out of this.
RONNIE:	With pleasure – but can you?

Ronnie adopts the persona of *Ryan's* mother.

RONNIE:	(*Mam*) Who's that at the door now?
RYAN:	Nobody! Just...
RONNIE:	(*Mam*) There was somebody at the door!
RYAN:	Bloke! Wanted to see me!
RONNIE:	(*Mam*) At my door!
RYAN:	Work! Next month, maybe. It's not important!

RONNIE: (*Mam*) Work! On the Sabbath!

RYAN: No! Friday evening!

RONNIE: (*Mam*) May I remind you that this is my house, and that today is the day of the Lord!

RYAN: May I ... remind you ... that I'm a married man with children now?!

RONNIE: (*Mam*) You're not too old to feel the back of my hand, my boy!

RYAN: Stop! (*Then to Ronnie*) Stop. That's so ... cheap.

RONNIE: Come round and see my mother and I'll show you...! (*Pauses*) Sorry.

RYAN: When I walk through the door it'll be the same old story. Could've opened in Vegas for all she cares, just like Tom Jones. (*American in the persona of Willie Clark*) Tom Jones is gonna get a hundred thousand dollars a week in Las Vegas! When Lewis and I were headlining at the Palace, the *Palace* didn't cost a hundred thousand dollars! All of that, and it would still be 'wipe your feet before you come in!' 'Have you eaten?' 'Are you spending time with your wife and children?' 'When are you going to get a proper job?' 'The rubbish needs taking out the back!' Why? What do I have to do to become more than just 'family'?

Ryan and *Ronnie* re-engage.

RONNIE: If BBC London want six fifty-minuters at prime time, then they'll have to take a little bit of shit with it. It's OK, Ry! I've got it in hand!

RYAN:	What's that then, Ron – the one bird? I'm worried about the other two, lurking in the bush!
RONNIE:	Don't be; I'm on top of it.
RYAN:	Must be a bird.
RONNIE:	(*Dictaphone*) I've got the machine.
RYAN:	Won't it go up on its own?
RONNIE:	I'm up at six; by seven, the machine's full.
RYAN:	Do we post it to Billy Cotton?
RONNIE:	Fuck him. Do what you like.
RYAN:	You can't indulge in sexual activities with Billy Cotton, cariad; it's against the law. Well, not without his written permission anyway.
RONNIE:	I can make it, once I'm home and settled. (*To dictaphone*) Have a bottle of vodka waiting for me when I get there!
RYAN:	What will the doctor say?
RONNIE:	Do you want it straight, Mr Williams, or with tonic? (*Re dictaphone*) Very latest, see? Like a mini tape recorder, only better. You can take it with you anywhere! I've bought ten of them, one for every room!
RYAN:	Does it write on its own? Can you get me one?
RONNIE:	I can get you ten.
RYAN:	Boom, boom.

RONNIE:	The toilet is very inspirational...!
RYAN:	Twyfords?
RONNIE:	I sit there for hours! It goes directly from my head into this miraculous machine!
RYAN:	Not down the pan?
RONNIE:	It's the answer to our prayers, Ry!
RYAN:	Amen! (*He puts an imaginary telephone to his ear*) Mr Cotton, sir? It's all systems go down in Gwalia fach! I've got a man 'ere with ten machines, working his arse off! (*Aside to Ronnie*) Can't say 'arse' on English television! Maybe we should keep Pete and Bob sweet, Ron – just in case.
RONNIE:	I'm not listening.
RYAN:	Robinson and Hedley: could be the real answer to our prayers! They're certainly a couple of names to conjure with.
RONNIE:	Are we joining the magic circle?
RYAN:	Two of the finest writers in television comedy today!
RONNIE:	What about tomorrow? Can they come back next week?
RYAN:	This week, Ron! We need them this week! We need them now!
RONNIE:	*You* ... need them!! Like blood to a tiger, you need them so much it's killing you!

RYAN:	(*Tough sergeant major*) So! You want to join the army, eh? (*Very effeminate*) Yes…!! (*Sergeant*) Could you kill a man? (*Effeminate, after appropriate pause*) Eventually!!
RONNIE:	Could I see Ryan Davies – citizen – for a minute, please?
RYAN:	Ron, if we make a success of this, people will say: at least they can get away from that parochial thing!
RONNIE:	But ... why would we want to?
RYAN:	Don't get me wrong! I'd still be keen to keep one foot in Wales!
RONNIE:	How the hell did 'we' become 'I' all of a sudden? In such a short space of time!
RYAN:	Ah! The magic of showbiz!
RONNIE:	And what about this foot, eh? Which foot are we planning on keeping in Wales then – the gammy one, is it? And put the best foot forward – to England and beyond?
RYAN:	Beyond! Up, up and away!
RONNIE:	On that bloody silver ship I suppose! Seems to me there's room for only the one! (*He calms down a bit; tries to be reasonable*) What's the point in being small fishes in England...?
RYAN:	And beyond!
RONNIE:	When we can be really big fishes back home in Wales?
RYAN:	And get to where, Ron?

RONNIE:	Bristol Channel?

They laugh spontaneously.

RONNIE:	Tell me, Ry – what would you like on your grave?
RYAN:	'I'd rather be playing Port Talbot'?
RONNIE:	Ryan Davies, citizen, please?
RYAN:	Oh, I don't know. Just 'Ryan' I suppose.
RONNIE:	(*Resigned*) Lucky sod.

Light change. Music – theme to Tom Jones' 'Delilah'. Buzz of an expectant audience. **Ryan** *and* **Ronnie** *appear in a half light. They are waiting to go onstage.* **Ronnie** *is very nervous,* **Ryan** *is clearly unwell; every breath is a struggle.*

RYAN:	'To be – or not to be: that is the question: whether tis nobler in the mind to suffer the slings and arrows of outrageous fortune, or to take arms against a sea of troubles, and by opposing end them? To die: to sleep ...'
RONNIE:	What's that...?
RYAN:	That, Ronnie, is Mr Shakespeare.
RONNIE:	I know who he is. How the hell did he get here is all I'm asking!
RYAN:	The old discipline. It works for me. 'To die: to sleep...'
RONNIE:	No more!
RYAN:	'And by a sleep to say we end...'

RONNIE:	'...this fucking nightmare; this'
RYAN:	'Heartache and the thousand natural shocks that flesh is heir to.'
RONNIE:	You're not, are you?!
RYAN:	Might have to, boi, the state you're in!
RONNIE:	You do, and I'll kill you! You dare go off script with that rubbish…!

Pause.

RYAN:	I can't make it.
RONNIE:	What did you say?
RYAN:	I can't go on; and that's the biggest admission of my life.
RONNIE:	Exactly what I told my doctor this afternoon!
RYAN:	I mean it!
RONNIE:	*I* meant it!
RYAN:	(*He fears the worst*) What?
RONNIE:	I went to see my doctor.
RYAN:	(*Doesn't want to face it*) Doctor, doctor – I think I'm a pair of curtains! What do you advise?
RONNIE:	Pull yourself together, man. Boom bleeding boom.
RYAN:	Seriously?

RONNIE:	Seriously, seriously?
VOICE OVER TANNOY:	Ladies and gentlemen...!
RYAN:	Start without me.
RONNIE:	You must be fucking joking!
VOICE OVER TANNOY:	Please give a warm, Double Diamond welcome...!
RYAN:	Not this time, cariad.
VOICE OVER TANNOY:	To Ryan and Ronnie!!

Music; applause. **Ronnie** *stumbles into the full light.* **Ryan** *stays in the half light.*

RONNIE: Thank you! Thank you! Well ... what can I say? He was right behind me, honest!

He gets a decent laugh. It gives him confidence.

RONNIE: He'll be here now – in a minute!

Another respectful laugh.

RONNIE: Any second now! (*He pauses*) Heard the one about Siencyn and Myfanwy? No? Well, it's bloody good! Even the band laughed! Very rare, I can tell you!

But the laughs are getting thinner; he is floundering.

RONNIE: Hang on...!

*He goes and picks **Ryan** up in his arms. Returns to the full light. Applause.*

RYAN: 'Allo 'ow are yew? W, I'm bad! I'm baaard, I am! Don't laugh, Mrs Prosser bach! Been to see the doctor and everything! Gave me a lovely diagnosis, he did! Gave me some medicine as well!

Sporadic laughter throughout the above, climaxing in big laughter at the end.

RYAN: 'Ere! 'Eard the one about Siencyn and Myfanwy? No? Well, it's bloody good! Even the band laughed! Very rare, I can tell you!

Big laughter.

RYAN: (*Through gritted teeth*) Got 'em! Put me down! Put me *down*!

***Ronnie** puts **Ryan** down to applause.*

RYAN: You weren't expecting me tonight, were you? Neither was I to tell you the honest truth, myn uffarn i!

*More laughter. **Ryan** is in complete control. **Ronnie** seems totally impotent.*

RYAN: (*Re Ronnie*) And neither was he, if that face is anything to go by!

Laughter.

RYAN: Look out! He's going to ask me something...! Look out, 'ere it comes!

*But **Ronnie** seems frozen to the spot, his grin fixed.*

RYAN: Don't you want to know what happened next, Ron?

RONNIE: No. Yes! What happened next, Ry?

RYAN: Oh, this boy's a genie...!

*Laughter – but **Ryan** is willing **Ronnie** to give him the 'feed'.*

RONNIE: Oh! Uh ... don't you mean 'genius'?

RYAN: I 'aven't got a clue, bach, it was so long ago!

RONNIE: (*Doggedly*) Don't ... you ... mean ... 'genius'?

RYAN: (*Taking the piss*) 'Ave ... a ... rub ... see ... what ... you ... think!

*It's **Ryan** that gets the laugh. **Ronnie** is rooted to the spot. **Ryan** takes centre stage, leaving **Ronnie** marginalised.*

RYAN: Oh, it's lovely to be back! No, I tell a lie, I've never been 'ere before, so how the 'ell can I be back?! Seriously for a minute – the wife said to me the other day; she said: 'I'd like a holiday; I'd like to go somewhere I haven't been to before.' I said: 'Try the kitchen!'

*Laughter. During the above, **Ronnie** backs out of the light and finally goes off.*

RYAN: Oh look, a piano! Who put that by there now…? Shall we have a little song?

*Applause. **Ryan** goes to the piano.*

RYAN: Reiti-ho! Ready?

He slams his fingers down – but the lid is closed. He takes a while to 'realise' this.

RYAN: 'She...!
May be the face I can't forget
A trace of pleasure or regret...!'
Oops! Sorry! Why din' yew tell me…?!

He lifts the lid up.

RYAN: Oh, look! 'Ave a butcher's at this! Some of the keys 'ave gone all mouldy and black! Ych a fi!

Laughter.

RYAN: Only jokin'!

He carries on playing and singing – badly – à la Les Dawson.

RYAN: 'May be my treasure or the price I have to pay
She may be the song that summer sings
May be the chill that autumn brings
Within the measure of the day...!'

But gradually, he moves away from the 'jokey' interpretation until the song is sung perfectly.

RYAN: 'She
May be the beauty or the beast
May be the famine or the feast
May turn each day into heaven or a hell
She may be the mirror of my dreams
A smile reflected in a stream
She may not be what she may seem
Inside a shell...'

Big applause.

RYAN: I'd like to finish off with a Welsh song. It's one of my
                  favourites...

                  'Holl amrantau'r sêr ddywedant
                  Ar hyd y nos,
                  Dyma'r ffordd i fro gogoniant
                  Ar hyd y nos,
                  Golau arall yw tywyllwch
                  I arddangos gwir brydferthwch,
                  Teulu'r nefoedd mewn tawelwch
                  Ar hyd y nos...'

*During the singing of the above, the light gradually fades on **Ryan** and
comes up on **Ronnie** in a very despondent mood.*

Applause.

Ryan *joins* **Ronnie**.

RYAN: What are you ... really, really saying?

RONNIE: You know what I'm saying.

RYAN: (*American*) We got back to the dressing room, he took
                  off his make-up, put his clothes on and said to me:

RONNIE: Don't do that!

RYAN: (*American*) He said:

RONNIE: That's what I'm saying!

RYAN: (*American*) Willie, if it's all the same to you, I'm retiring.
                  (*Himself*) What?

RONNIE:	That! That ... awful accent. It's typical of the lie we're living.
RYAN:	(*American*) Excuse me? (*Himself*) What's wrong with it?
RONNIE:	Nothing! I'm talking about the lie.
RYAN:	Your accent is terrible!
RONNIE:	It doesn't matter! It's not going anywhere! Look, it's ... just not you, Ry.
RYAN:	'You' or 'yew'?
RONNIE:	Well ... exactly. It's a big decision you have to make. Will it be laverbread or lavender, cawl or caviar?
RYAN:	Woa! Wait a minute...
RONNIE:	Me? Do they have tonic proper, or will I have to slum it with slimline?
RYAN:	Without you – is that what you mean? Is that what you mean, Ron?! Is this ... a sketch?
RONNIE:	It's life.
RYAN:	Is that ... what the doctor said?
RONNIE:	He said, 'You can't get ten pounds of shit into a five-pound bag.' No, I made that up. He said:
RYAN:	Let's have a holiday! Recharge the old batteries, what d'you say? Sun, sea, sangria!

RONNIE:	Aeroplane's full, Davies. Missed it, anyway. Look, we've been incredibly lucky, agreed?
RYAN:	Luck? What's that got to do with anything? It's all about talent and hard work! And never taking your foot off the peddle.
RONNIE:	That's you in a nutshell!
RYAN:	Think so? Do you honestly think I've got what it takes to make it?
RONNIE:	Don't spoil it.
RYAN:	No, listen...! People might say it: you know, our public, the common herd and barbarous multitude, ife Ron, as Shakes would have it – but what do you think?
RONNIE:	Even now, after seven years? Still needs a massage, does it?
RYAN:	Difficult though, innit...!
RONNIE:	I'm not going to say it!
RYAN:	We ... ourselves ... can never be objective.
RONNIE:	That's a big word for a West Walian!
RYAN:	I've been practising!

*There is a suggestion of a faint smile between them – but **Ronnie** hardens again.*

RONNIE:	I'm not going to give you the satisfaction!

Ryan – bless him – can't help it: he has to do a quick take on Mick Jagger.

RYAN: 'I ... can't get no ... satisfaction!'

RONNIE: You want me to tell you how good you are, but I'm not going to oblige!

RYAN: *You're* good! Hell, I couldn't have done it without you, bach!

RONNIE: Don't make me laugh.

RYAN: I make you laugh? That's terrific; it's all I wanted to hear!

RONNIE: Boom, boom.

RYAN: So...! Are we OK? Tell me we're OK! Tell me I was right to turn my back on Shirley Primary, Croydon.

Ronnie remains silent.

RYAN: Oh, there we are then...! Go back to announcing, if that's what you want. Weren't you a bus conductor once?

RONNIE: Don't talk to me about careers! School radio? Pardon me while I faint! 'Sgubor bleedin' Lon'? (*He slaps his thigh to the rhythm*):
'O, ffwl la la, ffwl la la, ffwl la la, la la la la!'
God, give the man a biscuit!

Ryan becomes very angry. He grabs Ronnie by the lapels.

RONNIE: Yes, dear, what is it?

RYAN: It's called 'Welshness', Ron – your 'ffwl la la'. Treftadaeth, gw'boi! It's our heritage!

RONNIE: It's morris dancing with a double 'f'!

RYAN: If you do...! If you do, Ron, people will say:

RONNIE: (*'Act'*) Tell me, Ryan...! Why the split?

RYAN: Doctor's orders: large vodka and slimline tonic! (*Re Ronnie's drink*) He's already on medication as you can see!

RONNIE: What did the doctor actually say?

RYAN: Keep taking the tablets, or Smirnoff condensed in your case!

RONNIE: See, boys? I can't compete with genius like that!

RYAN: Don't you mean 'genie'?

*Ronnie drops the act; he considers **Ryan** fondly.*

RONNIE: 'Ave a rub, butt – see what you think.

Both are emotional.

RYAN: If you do ... not only are you letting my wife and children down – not only are you letting your *own* wife and children down – not to mention the whole of Wales – but you are letting my fucking *mother* down, gw'boi!

RONNIE: That's a big word for a West Walian.

RYAN: Mother?

Another fond look between them.

RYAN:	What ... in the name of Judas do I tell *her*? That I'm a one-bone dog now? That I'm up shit creek without the proverbial paddle? That Siôn has lost his Siân?
RONNIE:	'Methinks the lady doth protest too much.'
RYAN:	Oh, look – it's the Davies boy! He's home, and he's ... he's ... what's 'waglaw' too?
RONNIE:	Empty-handed.
RYAN:	That's it! That's what they'll say! 'Look, he's like all the others – quite ... ordinary.' 'Here comes Shane,' they'll say ... 'with his tail between his legs.' 'Didn't beat Jack Palance to the draw after all.' 'Look, he's off to work! He's catching the seven thirty-five for some dreary, spotlight-forsaken comp. Superb teacher, they do say! Inspirational! And funny? Why, only the other day he surprised his own wife by turning up wearing a police-man's uniform! Had his back to the front door when she opened it; nearly had a seizure, she did! My word, what an original talent! No doubt about it, he's a legend in his own household, that man! He should be on stage, or something...! Just like ... Rab Butler, the greatest prime minister we never had, and all that palaver. You know – this is the bed Henry VIII would have slept in had he not stayed in the house over the road.' Who the hell wants to be on the *edge* of history, Williams?
RONNIE:	Don't go home – go on. You're free, Davies – can't you see?

Ronnie picks up the silver ship.

RONNIE:	Free, to sail into uncharted waters. Rightly or wrongly, it's what you must do. I'm an useless sailor, bach! You'd be forever bailing me out!

RYAN:	Free?

RONNIE:	They're waiting for you, Ry.

A long, affectionate look between them as the light changes. **Ryan** *goes off, singing lightly.*

RYAN:	'Ar lan y môr, mae rhosys cochion Ar lan y môr, mae lilis gwynion ...' etc.

Light change; on **Ronnie** *now, clutching the silver ship.*

RONNIE:	Back on the boards: the odd dodgy play in my native tongue; a few cameos for TV and film. *Twin Town*. Quite enjoyable. Had twins in it ... or something. For my last scene, I had to conduct a funeral at sea. Ironic, that.
Pause.	

RONNIE:	Spot of announcing (*BBC voice*): Good evening, this is the news: the American film actor Steve McQueen has died, aged fifty. By common consent, his last coherent words, in Spanish, were 'lo hice' – 'I made it.'

Ronnie *runs a hand over the silver ship thoughtfully.*

RONNIE:	I ... made it.

Pause.

RONNIE:	Sure I heard the news – hasn't everybody in Wales? Where were you when Kennedy was shot? When Armstrong walked the moon? Just the solitary name, like Twiggy or Topol. Heard the news? (*He becomes very, very emotional*) I'm going to hear it for the rest of my bloody life!!! (*He composes himself*) This bloke ... he phones me up; this tosser gets in touch, and he says to

RONNIE:
(continued)

me: 'He was booked to appear on the ninth; the posters have been printed, the tickets have been sold – what do I do?' So I said: 'Do you want the lend of a fucking shovel?!'

The song, 'With My Little Pick and Shovel' creeps in under the remainder.

RONNIE:

No, on second thoughts, he took the shovel with him, long time ago. From the moment he was born...

*During the last bit, **Ronnie** has been slowly crushing the silver ship into a featureless lump.*

*Light change. **Ronnie** goes off. **Ryan** comes on in a white DJ.*

RYAN:

Dear Ron, I'm in awe – a small village, just outside Merthyr. I tell a lie, I'm in front of the Lincoln Memorial. Dew, he's the spitting image of me, aye! All sad ... and serious. People say that I'm a sad and serious little man; even my best friends say it! But then ... comedy is a sad and serious business.

That Abraham Lincoln fella, they do say he had Welsh blood! (*American*) Heck, doesn't every American? Had he lived ... he would've been about a hundred and fifty years old now! Happy birthday to yew, happy birthday to yew! He might even have paid the old country a visit – you know, 'gwlad y menyg gwynion' ife! Land of the white gloves, Ron, that's what some do call it! Anyway, here I am, doin' the reverse of what dear old Abe never had the the chance to do – (*American*) – 'will that be a taxi for *one*, Mrs Lincoln? Ron ... if you think Ammanford's big – well think again! This place is called Buffalo, but do you know, I haven't seen one of the critters yet! Plenty of room to hide, see? Weather changeable; bit like Wales, really. Snow ... followed by intense heat and humidity.

Ryan pauses, he is having difficulty breathing.

RYAN: Not yet. Jesus Christ, have a heart. There's one more song to sing.

Light change. Ronnie comes on in a white DJ.

RYAN: Williams, mun! What kept you?

RONNIE: Took me a while to find the right bridge!

RYAN: Ouch! That's a bit cheap!

RONNIE: Come round to see the bridge...!

RYAN/RONNIE: And I'll show you cheap! Boom, boom!

RYAN: Never mind, you're here now!

RONNIE: It's now or never!

RYAN: I can feel a song coming on!

RONNIE: Oh, no – not another bloody song!

RYAN: Hey – you can't use that word up 'ere, gw'boi!

RONNIE: Song?

Both smile.

RYAN: Don't worry about it! Let's just say ... we're in a bar.

RONNIE: Bar! Now you're talking.

RYAN: There's a piano in the corner...!

Ryan goes to the piano and starts tickling the ivories.

RONNIE: A bar; piano! And just the two of us?

RYAN: Not just the two of us, Ron. There's all our friends.

RONNIE: Really?

RYAN: All out by there – see?

Ryan nods to actual audience.

RONNIE: (*Fondly*) Well a jiw jiw! Look...! There's...!

RYAN: No! Don't embarrass them. Just ... be you. Remember?

RONNIE: Is that all?

RYAN: That's all they want.

RONNIE: Be me? Right! Pa nosweth yw hi, Ry? What night is it? Where we playing?

RYAN: Ron – I'm glad you asked me that! It's every night of the week for the rest of their lives, gw'boi! And you know what that means don't you?

RONNIE: Easier to get to heaven than get a North Walian to smile?

RYAN: Close! Myn uffarn i, close!

A moment, as both reflect. Intro music to 'Myfanwy.'

RYAN/RONNIE: 'Paham mae dicter, O Myfanwy
Yn llenwi'th lygaid duon di
A'th ruddiau tirion, O Myfanwy
Yn gwrido wrth fy ngweled i
Pa le mae'r wên oedd ar dy wefus
Fu'n cynnal cariad ffyddlon ffôl
Pa le mae sain dy eiriau melys
Fu'n denu'm calon ar dy ôl...

Pa le mae sain dy eiriau melys
Fu'n denu'm calon ar dy ôl...'

Big applause as the lights go.

THE END